The Profitable & Stress-Free Eye Doctor

The
Profitable &
Stress-Free
Eye Doctor

The Step-by-Step Guide to Grow a
Successful Ortho-K Specialty Business

DR. CONNIE VUONG

NEW YORK

LONDON • NASHVILLE • MELBOURNE • VANCOUVER

The Profitable & Stress-Free Eye Doctor

The Step-by-Step Guide to Grow a Successful Ortho-K Specialty Business

© 2020 Dr. Connie Vuong

Published in New York, New York, by Morgan James Publishing in partnership with Difference Press. Morgan James is a trademark of Morgan James, LLC. www.MorganJamesPublishing.com

ISBN 9781642797565 paperback
ISBN 9781642797572 eBook
Library of Congress Control Number: 2019948293

Cover Design Concept:
Jennifer Stimson

Cover & Interior Design by:
Christopher Kirk
www.GFSstudio.com

Editor:
Todd Hunter

Book Coaching:
The Author Incubator

Morgan James is a proud partner of Habitat for Humanity Peninsula and Greater Williamsburg. Partners in building since 2006.

Get involved today! Visit
MorganJamesPublishing.com/giving-back

"Who dares to be on the top of the highest mountain where the most powerful thunder hits and the strongest wind blows? Only a tiny and oblivious flower!"
– Connie Vuong

The book is dedicated to a great visionary who believed that his little girl is capable of anything she sets her mind on. I was very fortunate to be able to sit on a giant's shoulder, my dad's. You have foreseen a bright future for me on that afternoon when I was 16; planning my future with you in our backyard. I can still picture a young daughter and a wise father. Without hesitating or thoughts, you said that I should be an eye doctor. You have shaped my unimaginable future. I am forever grateful to you, Dad.

Table of Contents

Foreword

Dr Connie Vuong focuses on what it takes not only to make patients who need a spectacle correction happy & glasses free but also to transform the eye doctor's practice to one of financial freedom & increased time for family, relaxation, & special interests

Indeed, we are made to understand there is a worldwide myopia epidemic & it is important for each practitioner to be able to meet the challenge in their offices by advising & treating patients with such an effective myopia control modality such as orthokeratology.

Dr Vuong seamlessly navigates each doctor down the path of orthokeratology as a specialty with guidance on attracting

& selecting potential patients. She advises the reader on promoting Orthok in the community through mass media outreach which she has mastered. In addition, there is a valuable list of resources in her book to help secure Orthok success.

Dr Vuong allows us to understand her philosophy of Work Less- More Free Time Schedule which can be a reality through making the world better -2 eyes at a time -with myopia control & orthokeratology.

Dr Robert Grand
Author, THE COSMIC CARROT
A children's picture book

Chapter 1:

The Realization

"Even paradise could become a prison if one had
enough time to take notice of the walls."
– Morgan Rhodes, Falling Kingdoms

The Challenges Eye Doctors Are Now Facing

As an eye doctor, you entered optometry with the highest confidence that you will change many lives with your professional care. You perform eye examinations to detect, diagnose, and then treat your patients' conditions.

These patients accept your recommendations and they return to you for further care. Now more than ever before, eye care providers face challenges that are slowly endangering their existence.

Patients are utilizing their insurance, pay copays, getting their eye exams, and they leave your office. On their way out, they ask for a copy of the prescription so they can order glasses and contact lenses online. Over time you are noticing that most patients are coming in just for the exams. Your income has been significantly reduced compared to just a few years prior. Just the other day, you heard a colleague say that there is an app that just came out where patients can look at their phone and the app will measure their eyeglasses prescription for them. Patients also start looking online to self-diagnose their eye conditions. They no longer need you as their eye care provider. On top of that, your local competitors started to give massive discounts to attract more patients to their office. You think to yourself, "Should I do the same?" What a dilemma!

The Story of a Disillusioned Eye Doctor

Graduation day was one of the best days of your life! Now, finally, you are ready to spread your wings of knowledge and go out into the world and change lives for the better. You received one of the highest badges of honor, the title of doctor. Your chest almost exploded with pride. Your parents' teary eyes told the whole story – they were proud beyond words! So joyful, they probably could not sleep for days.

You were so confident that you would help more people by having your very own practice. You called it, "My Baby!" The grand opening of your baby, your practice, was one of the most memorable days of your life! Friends and family members came. They used their insurance, ordered eyeglasses, and paid for all the services. They referred their friends and co-workers. Your practice was a buzzing place of excitement. "Life is great!" you thought to yourself.

One day, two years after you had that special day, you came to work and noticed your office is not buzzing but were much quieter. Maybe things were settling down. Maybe it was just slow because of tax season. It will pick up you thought to yourself. Unwilling to accept it that business had been slowing down, you started to count the number of years. It has been like this for the last four years! How long will this still be going on? What will happen if this scenario was left alone to run its course? Closing the door to your practice would feel like letting it die a painful death.

For some time, it was me who had been going through the scenario I laid out above. I, too, had been there and done that. Only my agony was much longer than four years. I needed to set my stubbornness aside and start facing the fact that things needed to change. I needed to face my fears to save My Baby! Are you willing to do the same?

Face the Fear and Go into Action

If practicing general optometry is all you have been accustomed to you may be asking yourself these questions:

"What else can I do? Do I have to start over?

Do I have to learn a new skill for this new specialty? Where do I find the time?

Do I need to invest in more expensive equipment?

How do I find all those new patients?

Am I good enough?"

Questions that raise concerns race through your brain. You almost feel an anxiety attack coming on. You see, the more you worry the more you realize that you cannot stay in your current situation. The longer you wait, the more you are mentally exhausted thinking about the terrible situation you are in. As time goes on, resources will run low and your financial situation will worsen. You might need to sell your business or go work for someone. You might even need to close the practice and just walk away from it. Thereafter, you will never be able to look back on living the dream of being an entrepreneur.

There are, however, actions you can take to change. First, you got to change your mindset. You were trained on so many different specialties while in professional school. You have those skills already. You just need to put them into the right gear. Second, there are numerous eye doctors who have extremely successfully transitioned from practicing general to specialty optometry. Plan to be part of the specialty academy that you can start your training with. There are mentoring and coaching programs that can assist you to start your journey. You do not have to do this alone. Thirdly, after all the right foundation is set into its rightful place, you can with confidence start recommending your specialty to all nearsighted patients. These patients will appreciate the much-needed service that you offer. Once they have enjoyed the benefits of clear vision, they will start recommending you to their family and friends. Before you know it, you will be known as the expert and your practice will thrive.

Reap the Reward

Here is a glimpse of what your career and private life would be like once your specialty service is fully implemented in your happy-centered practice. You get to choose the days and the hours you can see your patients. It is possible to see patients only on three half-days. Each half-day consist of three to four hours of work a day. This will total at nine to sixteen hours per week. When compared with your general optometry practice, you will see fewer patients but earn significantly more. By providing the much-needed concierge type of specialty services, patients are willing to pay out of pocket with the amount that is comparable to orthodontics services. With so much extra free time, you will be able to enjoy more quality time with your loved ones.

The Successful Strategies Within This Book

Step-by-step proven strategies are detailed within this book. These strategies are the strong foundation for the building block of achieving a successful specialty practice. Once the decision is made to provide specialty Ortho-K therapy, success is just around the corner. When deciding to build an Ortho-K specialty practice, knowing all the right reasons for the service and the benefits is critical. Learning the effective skills to deliver the message of how dangerous the myopia epidemic is can effectively change lives. Parents will readily choose your Ortho-K program to save their children's eyesight. You will become familiar with how and where to obtain the proper instruments and equipment for your patients' optimum outcome. You will gain the skills of knowing which Ortho-K lens companies are best suited for any type of eye conditions. Detailed techniques on teaching patients the Ortho-K lens care will be taught and mastered by you and all your staff personals. The flow of Ortho-K patients' service will be shown to you in easy, practical steps. By putting the continuum of care in your practice, you will ensure a profitable practice for years to come. Ultimately, your greatest reward in your career life is making sight-saving contributions to so many young lives.

Chapter 2:

My Solution of Giving the Gift of Sight

*"Strength and growth come only through
continuous effort and struggle."*
– Napoleon Hill

I remember that summer day so vividly! I turned 16 and I just survived a major car accident! That Monday, I passed my driver's test and right away on that Friday, I drove my friends to the movie theatre. On the way there, as I was turning left at an intersection, I heard a loud crash. Thereafter, I was unconscious for a few minutes. When I woke up my car was totaled. Kaput! I realized that my vision was so weak that I did not see the oncoming car as I was turning left. After the car accident, my dad took me to an eye doctor. She said that my vision was 20/400, with a prescription of -3.00.

I was heart-broken! Not only did I damage my first car beyond repair, I also found out that my eyes were so bad that I will be depending on glasses for the rest of my life. My dad was very calm. He was not upset. He turned this dilemma into an opportunity for me. He said, "What if other kids are like you? Can't see and they don't even know it? What if you could bring awareness about eye care and prevention? You should work toward a goal to service others like you." At the age of 16, I started my journey toward the goal of bringing awareness and hopefully prevention of nearsightedness/myopia to children.

Like many eye care providers, I started out providing general optometric services to my patients. These included eye exams, glasses, and contact lenses. The main source of income came from vision insurance companies. Since I started my practice from scratch, there weren't a lot of patients. Most of my patients then found me through vision insurance company directories and Medicaid services. When starting a practice "cold," you need to have patience for business to pick up and grow over time. In reality, during the first few years in practice, I found that there were many private practices, similar to mine, that were barely making enough to cover their expenses.

I worked at another practice to supplement the income. After a few years, my practice's revenue steadily increased and I was able to step away from the part-time job at the other practice. However, I noticed vision insurance companies started to cut their reimbursement to all their eye doctors. In addition, online companies selling glasses and soft contacts for significantly less started to pop up every second. Because of these things, my income was slowly declining with each passing year.

Facing the terrible fear of having to close my practice, I searched desperately for a solution. A call from a friend changed my life completely. Her radio guest speaker cancelled last minute. She thought of me and invited me on the talk show. We sat together to talk about different things in our lives on a live talk show. Somehow, the topic of nearsighted children came up. I told her that I helped my nieces control their nearsightedness with a specialty therapy called Ortho-K. To my surprise, when I got back to my practice, ten minutes later, my office was full of children wearing glasses. Parents wanted to have that specialty therapy for their children so desperately. Since that day, 98 percent of my patients are Ortho-K patients! These parents willingly pay out of pocket to save their children's eyesight. The initial stage of starting my Ortho-K was not without struggle. I had to face my insecurities about if I was the best doctor to provide this specialty care for these children. However, at that time, there weren't any doctors who offer this service. If I don't face my fear and insecurities and step forward and offer this healing therapy, who will?

For years, I continued doing my "homework" in the evening, read and re-read all the literature, and reviewed all the class notes on this topic I took in optometry school. I made numerous calls to all the Ortho-K lens designers ensuring that my patients get the best FDA approved lens material and designs. Day by day, my determination and passion grew. I knew that there is no better gift out there that parents can give their child but the gift of sight. I became so motivated to share this "Magic Therapy" that I wrote weekly articles, talked about it on TV shows and radio shows, held workshops and seminars to bring forth awareness of this sight-saving therapy. To this day, I can say that parents in the local area came to know me as the Pioneer Ortho-K Doctor. The years that followed were even more exciting for me.

At optometric continued education conference and conventions, whenever colleagues learned that I helped children with Ortho-K, they wanted to know more. During lunches and dinners with my colleagues, I would always hear them asking me about "How do you do this?" and "How do you do that?"

regarding Ortho-K therapy. Through many follow-up conversations via text messages and phones calls, I have been able to help my colleagues build their own successful Ortho-K practices. The goal of writing this book is to share my journey in building a specialty Ortho-K practice to even more eye care professionals.

Chapter 3:

The Successful Blueprint

Amazingly, it has been over a decade since I started my Ortho-K specialty practice. Since then so many changes have happened that I could hardly believe it. The majority of insurance companies were dropped. Our office consists of mainly Ortho-K patients; about 98 percent. I work about nine to sixteen hours per week. This leaves me with a lot of quality time to spend with my family. This is all possible due to the Successful Blueprint that I have created and perfected over the years. The realization that you already have the knowledge to start the journey of change toward Ortho-K specialty will be a huge step toward success.

Seven highly effective strategies will be detailed in a step by step process in the following chapters. Each of the following seven chapters will discuss the different but vital topics that will help you build a prosperous Ortho-K specialty practice. Chapter 4 discusses about the fact that you need to face the truth about the source of the eye doctor's problems. Then, solutions will be discussed to help eliminate insurance patients and focus more on quality patients rather than quantity through a high-class concierge service that shows your passion for myopic children. You will gain the skills to become known as the Ortho-K Guru. In Chapter 5, you will come to realize the power of your professional skill that you can offer to save so many youngsters' eyesight. If not you, then, who will step forward to provide such a critical sight-saving care? Once you focus on the benefits for these myopic children, your professional career will take on a new and much more meaningful experience. Be prepared to be passionate about your career again!

In Chapter 6, you will gain the confidence in delivering to parents the message that they yearn to hear; giving them hope and providing them with life-changing solutions. You will learn and share the useful tips and prevention to preserve the health of their eyes. In Chapter 7, you will learn the most effective ways to show your patients how action can speak louder through personal involvement with Ortho-K treatment by using the Ortho-K lens yourself. In Chapter 8, highly effective ways will be discussed on how to become known as the Ortho-K Guru in your area. In Chapter 9, the action starts! We will go step by step into how to implement the Blueprint in your newfound specialty practice. In Chapter 10, I am very excited to give you the secret on how to generate year after year "residual" income from Ortho-K patients you have successfully helped. In Chapter 11, we need to recognize the possible obstacles and learn ways to overcome them. In Chapter 12, we have completed our master blueprint plan; however, it does not end here. An exciting and fruitful journey has just begun. I am so excited to share my life's work with you and hope that you will have an amazing profitable and stress-free life as I have enjoyed for over a decade!

Chapter 4:

The Source of Eye Doctors' Problem

"Inaction breeds doubt and fear. Action breeds confidence and courage. If you want to conquer fear, do not sit at home and think about it. Go out and get busy."
– Dale Carnegie

Eliminate Insurance Plans

This is the question that represents the source of eye doctors' main concerns: How can we decrease our dependency on insurance companies for income? When I started my private practice, I was accepting all the insurance companies I could get my hands on. When a patient calls us to make an appointment, my staff had to check all the insurance companies to see which one they fall under, and then get the authorization for the service. The exam was performed. The staff assists the patient with the frame selection. The order was placed and the insurance was billed. If all went well, the payment would be received in two to three weeks after the service was rendered. When calculating all the time spent on the tasks just described, it's difficult to justify that time as being worthwhile. In order to have more time available to focus on the niche of Ortho-K therapy, insurance companies needed to be eliminated one by one.

Once you have reduced the time you spend on insurance-based patients, you will have plenty of time to focus on increasing your profitability. I started to make a list of all the insurance companies that we accept in our practice. Then, I started to list them in order of the most income it generated to the insurance companies that provide the least payment. As you have guessed already, VSP (Vision Service Plan) was our main bread-and-butter income. It provided the biggest check; 80 percent of all our earning came from VSP payments. We received only about 2-5 percent from Spectera Vision and about 10-15 percent from Davis Vision. After reviewing the statistics, I started to eliminate the insurances that reimburse the least (Spectera).

Next, I cut insurance (Davis Vision) that had too many criteria. With Davis Vision, a patient has to choose frames from Davis Vision's frame selection and all the eyeglasses' edging jobs had to be sent to them only.

On top of that, insurance companies tend to deny the claim for many medical conditions; requiring us to resubmit with a different diagnosis code. This not only wastes time but it also delays our reimbursement. And sometimes the insurance companies just deny any payment to us, stating that it is the responsibility of the patient. Now, we have to chase after the patient for the money. Good luck with that, right?

When you've played this game long enough, you will grow old fast trying to gain the upper hand. Therefore, we have to eliminate insurance from our practice! In order to fly high, you've got to cut the strings that chain you to normalcy. Once the patients from the insurance companies slowly decrease from your practice, you have more time to attend to the patients that really need your expertise. Only then can you enjoy more free time and have a profitable practice.

Quality over Quantity

Shouldn't you see as many patients as possible? Wouldn't that increase your bottom line? To answer these questions, some math might help. If the insurance company pays on average $100 for an eye exam per patient (the range is $50-$150) and we see 10 patients, you would make $1,000. If one specialty Ortho-K patient pays $2000 (the range is $2,000-$5,000; you take the lowest number here) and if there are 10 Ortho-K patients that month, an income of $20,000 is possible. In order to make $20,000 from the insurance companies, you would have to see 200 patients! What would you prefer, seeing 200 patients or 10 patients? Can you now see how this could free up so much more time? This extra time is plentiful; available for you to lavish your Ortho-K patients with special attention. Parents love the one-on-one consideration their children get from you, their very own Ortho-K doctor. During lens insertion and removal classes, the children get their own individual trainer that concentrates all his or her time on them. They will enthusiastically share this experience with other parents and this will lead to more referrals, thus more new Ortho-K patients. Just picture this. Soon, your specialty practice will be filled with only Ortho-K patients! Your practice has transitioned from a lifeless cocoon to a lively beautiful butterfly!

Passion for Myopic Children

Now, I know what you are thinking, of course, you want to see more specialty patients! But, can you build a practice consisting mostly of these kinds of patients? Yes, you need to develop an exceptional focus. You have already decided that you will be the Ortho-K expert in your area. Therefore, to be extreme, you got to breathe, think, and dream Ortho-K 24/7. This total mentality will not come to you right away. However, trust me, after you have successfully helped a child see 20/20 without wearing glasses, the first morning, you will be more excited than that parent or the patient. You will be mesmerized and addicted to the feeling of, "I did it! I improved another human being's life by saving their eyesight." You will never forget that face showing pleasant disbelief when your patient can see so clearly, HD (high depth) that you cannot stop thinking about it. It gives you enough gun-powder ammunition to want to improve, to move forward with your skills, to do more and be more for your patients.

Unknowingly, you slowly have adapted yourself to be the Ortho-K specialist who breathes, thinks, and dreams only of Ortho-K. Whenever you see a nearsighted patient or whenever you notice someone wearing glasses, your alert antennae will go up right away. You will start a serious discussion about the consequences and the danger of this epidemic condition with this person. You will provide them an effective myopic control FDA (Federal Drug Administration) approved solution. Parents can avoid you, can ignore you or run from you. But in the end, they will realize that their child can no longer see clearly, even with glasses on. Then, they will seek your guidance and care. Hopefully, that will happen sooner rather than later. In all my years in practice, I have sent three young patients to the Braille Institute of Blindness to apply for a guided dog. Each time, it felt like a sharp knife had punctured my heart. I felt helpless because their myopic condition had deteriorated beyond any hope. Each of these incidents kept me up many nights. This heart-sinking feeling made me work even harder in all aspects of Ortho-K patient care. I have developed an ambition to bringing forth awareness of this sight-robbing epidemic to as many people as possible so this will not happen to another child.

Emphasis on Concierge High-Quality Service

Give special attention to your Ortho-K patient. These patients will be seeing you 10-12 times per year. You and your team will be giving them one-on-one training on how to use the Ortho-K lenses, how to put those lenses in, and how to remove them all by themselves. You will provide them with instruction on how to sit (no slouching), what lighting to use during homework, what to eat, how long to study at one sitting, when to take breaks, etc. Their eye condition will be checked every four to eight weeks. During that time, they will be reminded about the tips and prevention methods for their eye condition. They will sit with their trainer again to learn the skills of keeping their eyes clean and healthy. When they have dry eyes, itchy eyes, red eyes, or even when their eyes feel "funny," you will make a same-day appointment to see them right away. Parents value this top-notch attentive care. Next thing you know, you have built a successful referral-based specialty practice because your patient's parents are voluntarily sharing your information with all their nieces, nephews, and friends.

Be Known as the Ortho-K Guru

Your name will be known as the local Ortho-K expert as parents share their awesome experience at your office to concerned parents. This means that it will be important to be consistent with your care. All children should be treated like they are your own children. You have effectively controlled their eye condition from getting worse. This way, parents will have peace of mind when their children are under your care. You need to provide an out-of-this-world service that the parents are convinced that the choice they made by coming to you is the best one they have ever made. You and your staff will be in constant communication with the parents should any concern arise. Your office will provide all the necessary information and services that that child needs to see clearly for a bright future.

Chapter 5:

Eye on the Benefits

"Only one who devotes himself to a cause with his whole strength and soul can be a true master. For this reason, mastery demands all of a person."
– Albert Einstein

There are millions and millions of parents out there who need your help. Each time they take their children to the eye doctor, they are afraid to hear bad news. They are afraid to ask the difficult question, but will have to ask it anyway: "Did my child's nearsighted prescription increase again this year?" Without waiting for your answer, they know the answer already. They just need you to confirm it. "Yes, your child's prescription has increased this year again." Immediately, you see the pain and sorrow in their eyes. For many years, these parents were searching for something that could potentially stop or slow down the progression of their child's myopic condition. They do not know if such a therapy exists. However, they are still desperately searching for any solution that could potentially stop the deterioration. They will continue their search. They will not give up. In fact, they are urgently seeking and needing your specialty Ortho-K. Who are you to deny them this care? You have to keep your eyes on the life-changing benefits you can provide for them.

After you have provided them with the Ortho-K therapy, these children will be able to see clearly without the need of their glasses. From then on, their nearsighted condition will be controlled effectively. They only need to wear the lenses at night to maintain the sharp vision during the day. The FDA approved Ortho-K therapy has been proven to slow or even stop the increase of nearsightedness in children. Why wouldn't you want to offer this revolutionary life-changing restoration to all of your patients? Wouldn't you want this for your own children? My nieces, nephew, and my daughter have been utilizing this convenient therapy – no daytime lenses or glasses for over 15 years. Their prescription has been stabilized since day one. You have a moral obligation and the professional duty to share this important message with as many parents as possible.

Chapter 6:

Total Focus on Myopia

"Thousands of candles can be lighted from a single
candle, and the life of the candle will not be shortened.
Happiness never decreases by being shared."
– Buddha

Myopia (nearsighted) is defined by Merriam-Webster as a condition in which the visual images come to a focus in front of the retina of the eye resulting especially in defective vision of distant objects.

Children and Myopia

A myopic individual cannot clearly see things at distance but is able to see them clearly up close. The image, that he or she sees, is not focused on the retina but it is focused in front of it.

The Brian Holden Institute's research indicated that by the year 2050, about five billion (half of the world's population) people will be affected by myopia. This epidemic can have a negative, life-altering impact on both the daily lives of those who suffer from it but also the people around them. In addition, the cost of health care rises out of proportion due to the increased risk of cataracts, glaucoma, retinal detachment, and myopic degeneration. All of these conditions can lead to irreversible vision loss. As an eye care provider, we got to be 100 percent focused in on intervening and educating these children. Early intervention is key. Parents need to place upmost priority on the frequent visits to an Ortho-K specialist to effectively control myopia.

Deliver the Message

How can you deliver the message that parents and patients should understand that it's critical to protect the eyes as soon as possible? Tell them a story that will touch their hearts yet creates fear that they could suffer a devastating fate if no action is taken urgently.

Below is a story of my accountant friend Peter whose vision is -5.00.

Peter: *"I need to tell you how frightening the last 6 months of my life have been!" "I took my kids to Disneyland. I went on one of the rides that they have there. When I got down, I noticed a dark cloud over my left eye. When I closed my right eye with my hand, I was shocked! I could not see anything out of my left eye! It was pitch black. Thereafter, I was taken to the eye doctor who referred me to a retinal specialist. I was diagnosed as having a tear in my retina! On the day of the surgery, as I was lying there waiting for the surgeon to come in, I thought of my wife and my two young kids. What if the surgery is not successful and I cannot continue to work? What will happen to us? Luckily, the surgery was a success. However, a couple of months later, at a follow-up visit, it was noted that the pressure inside my eyes was extremely high. The doctor told me that I have developed glaucoma! From now on, I will need to use pressure-lowering eye drops for the rest of my life. Four months later, the doctor gave me more bad news. He stated that I need to have another surgery. This time is to remove the cataract that had developed due to the complications from my high myopia condition."*

There is a takeaway in Peter's story which I have delivered in countless information sessions during parent-child conferences at my Ortho-K practice. Young myopes will carry this condition for the rest of their life. At a later time in life, the pathological effect of the condition is likely to manifest itself. Parents need to face the fact that if they do not change the way they care for their children's eyes now, the condition will worsen with each passing year. They already know this! This is the reason why they are sitting in my office today. This will be the same reason other parents will soon be sitting in front of you in your specialty Ortho-K practice; desperately needing your expertise.

Nature vs. Nurture

The first goal of the parent-child meeting is mainly to explain what causes myopia. I ask the young near-sighted patients if they know whether their grandparents are wearing nearsighted glasses or not. I ask them to look at their parents. Do they currently wear nearsighted glasses? Hearing those questions and knowing the answers, they would come the realization that they were not born with bad eyes, but those bad eyes were due to daily massive overuse or using them inappropriately.

Secondly, they need to understand that the development of myopia is likely linked to environmental factors. Research shows that decreased outdoor time can lead to increase in elongation of the eyeball. With an elongated retina, the image that this individual sees is projected further from the retina. The further it is from the retina, the higher the nearsighted prescription will be. Studies show that there is correlation between decreased time spend outdoors and increased in the eye's axial length. A study was conduct in Denmark where the number of hours of available sunlight varies greatly from 7 to 17.5 hours per day throughout the years. It shows that the rate of increase in myopia was significantly greater in the winter months than summer months. There have been several studies that were conducted with similar results.

Pro-longed near-work activities while using cellular phone, iPad, reading a book without frequent breaks can lead to muscle spasm within the eyes that can lock the flexibility mechanics of near-far viewing. In other words, the eyes are stuck after prolong usage at near and has difficulty relaxing to view distance object and see clearly. The majority of us were born with a perfect set of eyes; however, they did not come with an instruction manual. As eyecare specialist, we need to instill these important skills into our young patients' daily habits routine.

Wouldn't it be wise to have our children enjoy learning itself without imposing the academic competition? Parents often tell me that schools encourage children to read as much as possible. They will be rewarded by having their names display on the school's billboards. I am not surprised when mom told me that their child's name is always on top of that list. And they are over -6.00 nearsighted! The pressure that our educational school systems impose on our children could be the one of leading causes of their myopic condition.

I truly believe that by providing these children the sight saving skills and knowledge, to some extent, they can improve their current situation and control the outcome of their future eye condition. When implemented on a daily basis, these tips can lead to a highly desirable outcome.

Increased time in natural/sunlight outdoors at least 30 minutes per day is mandatory. Ergonomically, by holding the computer further out (20-24 inches) from the eyes can effectively lessen the strain on the eyes and decrease the eye fatigue. All of our Ortho-K patients in my clinic know the 20/20/20 rule by heart. For every 20 minutes of near work (reading, computer/ iPhone/iPad use), take 20 seconds breaks by looking at a distance of 20 feet. They have to look out at the trees, the car moving across, and breathe in and out slowly to release any tension. I am happy to report that the majority of our patients carry these excellent work/study habits into their adult lives, thus effectively stabilizing and preventing myopia from increasing.

Story of Tiana: Tiana started Ortho-K when she was 18 years old. She just graduated from high school. She got accepted to a Master science program at UC (University of California). Since her prescription is already -7.0, her parents were worried that it will increase significantly after 6 years of intense study. They started her on Ortho-K program with us that very summer. She left for college after successfully seeing 20/20. Armed with the knowledge of the Sight Preservation and of the 20/20/20 rule, not only was she able to prevent her prescription from increasing, but she was able to have a much lesser prescription after the six years of study there!

After you have shared numerous powerful, emotional, and caring stories, parents and children understand that you provide a sight-saving service that can significantly change their lives for the better. Therefore, they want to start the Ortho-K program with you that same day. They know waiting another day is not an option!

Giving Hope and Solution – Changing Lives!

For so many nights, you tossed and turned. Your mind is racing a thousand miles a minute hoping to find its home where your heart will be fully fulfilled. At the present, your career as an eye care professional leaves you with a sense of hopelessness. You know you were destined to provide value to others. However, you do not feel that you make a significant difference in other people's lives by selling eyeglasses. Deep down, you are convinced you can offer more and can make a huge contribution to others' lives. As an eye doctor, you are in luck, you can do so much. Saving sight can save lives! You only need to see the heart-warming appreciation in the parents' eyes once and you are convinced that providing Ortho-K specialty is your life's true calling!

Every day you will wake up, and you will be blessed with a new-found energy to change the future of yet another young child. By building an Ortho-K specialty practice, you can give hope to someone who felt hopeless for so many years seeing their child's eyes deteriorate beyond any solution in sight. Instead of answering, "Yes, your child's prescription has increased again" you now can firmly say, "no, her prescription did not increase this year. She can see 20/20 or better without glasses. The prescription has been stabilized!" With much pride, this is exactly the same sentence that has been echoing every day in my practice for so many years. What a relief for parents to hear!

Chapter 7:

Actions Speak Louder Than Words

"No one is useless in this world
who lightens the burdens of another."
– Charles Dickens

Your Credentials

You might think of credentials as your qualifications, achievements, diplomas, and awards. Yes, it's great to have all those things but what I am referring to as your credentials here are your words and actions. They are worth more than their weight in gold. As you sit in front of parents and the young myope, you describe an out-of-this world therapy.

However, can you truly know what you're talking about without experiencing it yourself? Therefore, the very first order of your successful business is that you must become your office's Ortho-K Patient Zero. Patient Zero is the patient that starts the whole new movement. You might say that this person starts a revolution. Who, other than you, would be best to lead this important mission?

The "Wow" Effect

Whether you are myopic, hyperopic, astigmatic, or presbyopic, you can benefit from the Ortho-K treatment. But it could happen that you do have perfect eyesight and you do not have any of the above conditions. That is even better. You see, Ortho-K is one of those procedures that the Ortho-K doctor has full control over. A custom design can be made to meet your needs. If you need to understand how a -3.00 myopic individual sees and lives his/her daily existence, then you can wear Ortho-K lenses that will simulate that for you. A +3.00 Ortho-K lens can be designed. After wearing it for one night, you distance will become 20/400. This is the blurred vision that an -3.00 individual experience. Only then, will you realize what this young person sitting in front of you feels. Amazingly, one of the biggest benefits is its reversible advantageous ability. As described earlier, after using a +3.00 lens for one night your vision will be 20/400. However, once you discontinue its use, your natural born eyes will reverse back to its natural state; 20/20 if you have perfect eyesight. Now, can you see why you've got to submerge yourself in these lenses to appreciate their powerful capabilities? Therefore, one needs to experience it to be able to describe the "wow" effect without any hesitation.

Thereafter, you can stand on solid ground in your awareness and can assist your patients successfully. As crazy as it may sound, before I fit a patient with any type of lenses, I wear them myself. For instance, when I see a patient who I prescribed a certain type of lenses; I order another pair for myself at the same time. When the lenses arrive at the office, I try them out. Sometimes I feel that they are great for me. However, most of the time, I feel I can't stand wearing them. At that moment, my heart goes out to these patients. And I go out of my way to make them feel as comfortable as possible. You see, they don't have many other choices. You can stop when you dislike wearing them. Yet, the patient needs to use these lenses daily to save their eyes. By seeing this from their perspective, you are now their compatriot sight-protector. There is no better way of ensuring a successful Ortho-K practice than being your practice's Patient Zero. By demonstrating trustworthy actions through genuine words, you have shown that the most powerful credentials are the ones that come from a pure heart.

Your Invaluable Front Line

As important as it is for you to be Patient Zero, your assistants in your office need to become Ortho-K patients themselves. A battle might be won by soldiers who believe in a mission half-heartedly. But to win a war against blindness, it is vital that all the generals and warriors rise together to combat a common foe. For me, it just so happened that my team all have bad eyesight or have a family member whose eyeglasses prescription is so high that they are at a serious risk of eye complications. With this kind of motivation, my team fights as hard as I do when they deliver education and training to patients. Every day we row in the same direction; this enables us to change so many young lives so successfully.

How can you assemble such a powerful team, your Invaluable Front Line? You have to make the staff trainings and meetings your highest priority. Heart-to-heart discussions with them must take place on a daily basis. I let them know that I could work for any doctor and still make a decent living. However, I chose to open a specialty practice where I can save children's eyesight so they can have a brighter future. They feel the pain the parents feel and they want to be part of this mission to alleviate it. You want them to feel the passion emanating from you. When you build a successful invaluable front line, your Ortho-K practice will be rewarded with endless possibilities.

The Unquestionable Positive First Impression

I heard that the client will make up their mind within the first 30 seconds they meet you. Thirty seconds is not a very long time. Your job is not to mess it up by contradicting that decision. Why would we want to convince them otherwise? We might do it unconsciously. You might be wearing thick glasses when you are supposed to be the expert in providing no- glasses therapy. A member of your staff wears glasses. The negative signals will slowly show up. The potential client starts to talk themselves out of starting therapy with you. "This doctor's eyes are so bad. She cannot even take care of her own eyes! How can she help my child? Her staff wears glasses. Obviously, she does not care enough to treat her own staff member!" On the contrary, if parents noticed that your office is well-equipped with the state of the art instruments and equipment, they are more like to feel confident that you are up to date with medical technology that can provide the optimal eye care. The biggest convincing factor is when they walk in your office and they often meet their relatives, friends, or classmates already doing therapy at your office!

Hard to believe but such occidental meetings do happen a lot in our office. The new family is instantly convinced; they will start therapy with you right away.

In order for parents and children to feel at ease with your office, all these factors need to be taken care of. When they walk into your office, do they notice other children who came in for follow-up care wearing glasses? 100 percent no! Do they see children sitting there with a trainer instructing them one-on-one? Yes, each patient gets their own trainer who devotes their full attention on that child. Do they see parents sitting there with a peace-of-mind smile on their relaxed face? Yes, all of them will proudly and happily tell their children's story of how their prescription has stabilized since coming here. In truth, the more you focus on caring whole-heartedly for these young patients' eyes, the more you are steadily building a heaven of individuals with healthy eyes. You, too, can create the unquestionable positive first impression by working on these essential fundamentals.

The Most Powerful and Valuable Testimonial

The most powerful and valuable testimonial parents will hear is not the one coming from any of your patients. It is the one parents hear coming from you. Having suffered from bad eyesight during my teenage years, I often endured ridicule from my classmates. I have been called four-eyes, "coke-bottled," a bookworm, and a nerd. I was always the last choice for the sports teams. Or I just ended up sitting in the corner most of the time during physical education classes. I was ecstatic when I was introduced to this magical nighttime-specialty lenses treatment, which I did not have to undergo any surgery for and did not require me to wear day-time soft contact lenses.

I am my practice's Patient Zero. The greatest story you can tell is your own story and that of your immediate family members. Parents become hopeful when they hear how you have a solution that saved your own eyesight. My prescription was -3.00. After utilizing Ortho-K, it is now only -0.75! That's a 66.6 percent reduction from my original prescription!

The parents relate to the emotional story of my young seven-year-old niece whose prescription increased threefold (from -1.00 to -3.00) in just 6 months. How amazing it is to have her prescription stabilize for the last 17 years. This leaves her to pursue any career dream she wishes without the hindrance of thick glasses or having any eye health complications later in life. Without needing to guess how high her prescription would be now if she had no Ortho-K, I can confidently say that she would have a double-digit prescription in the range of -10 or more.

The statement is based on the years of experience of seeing children increase one diopter per year. Also, this is based on the information from an actual patient whose parents did not allow their child to use Ortho-K. This patient just wears glasses and soft contact lenses. She also developed nearsightedness at the age of seven but now has a -11.00 prescription at the age of 25!

Many of my staff members are my Ortho-K patients who asked me if they could volunteer and work with me so that they could contribute; to give back and help spread the message of how devastating the myopic epidemic is. Their inspiration for this specialty is so great that many of them have gone on to pursue their own career path of becoming an eye doctor. We have a few staff members entering into the eye care professions. Currently, we have many Ortho-K patients interning at our office, training to follow my career path as well.

Of course, we are prideful when we hear stories our patients tell their friends about how they can see with no glasses, how their prescription has been under control ever since. Our Ortho-K parents share the sight-saving magical therapy to other parents while waiting at music lessons or sport events. Start creating your very own authentic valuable testimonials. You will be amazed at how it will spread like wild fire on a summer day.

The Acceptance of Care – A Call to Arms

The ultimate goal is to preserve children's eyesight. The most vital component to make this happen is your compelling trustworthy words and actions. In order for parents to place their children's eyes in your hands, they need to have the highest trust in you. Your "credentials" have to shine through to them. There is no doubt in their mind that you are passionate about what you do and that you will care with your heart. This is an enormous mission. How can you accomplish this mission if you are alone? You need the strongest team on your side, your valuable front line. Your staff is the critical surviving component of your Ortho-K practice. Do whatever you can to assemble your powerful sight-saving warrior team. Giving the best possible positive first impression will lead to agreement of service promptly. Your personal story must be included at every parent-patient conference. This will lead caring parents to take immediate action. All these vital elements will set their children off on their *See Clearly* journey.

Chapter 8:

Get Your Name Out There

"One customer, well taken care of, could be more valuable
than $10,000 worth of advertising."

– Jim Rohn

Word-of-Mouth Referral

One of the strongest and most effective forms of referral is the word-of-mouth referral. People are more likely to believe a customer than any other form of advertising. From my experience, this is the easiest way to gain more patients. The parents of these children come in, with their financial already prepared, ready to commit to start the Ortho-K program with you. You do not have to present any data or deliver your educational speech. Your patient's parents have delivered an exceptional lecture to them. This is all due to the fact that you have spent all the necessary time with them and have given these parents all the important information about the Ortho-K program. They have maintained that information and have shared it effectively. Your Ortho-K patient also acted as an educator for the new Ortho-K patient. Their excitement about this treatment comes through their voices. In order to enjoy all those benefits, the people that they share this amazing therapy with felt that they had to start it as soon as possible. If you try to talk them out of it, they respond, "No, my child has to start ASAP! I want the best medical procedure that is available for my child." "When will these Ortho-K lenses come in?" "Should I schedule the one-on-one training now?" They cannot contain their anxiousness to start the sight-saving program with you!

Educational Workshops

We hold monthly educational workshops. Each month, we invite a few of our favorite Ortho-K patients to attend. They are the patients who are so happy about the Ortho-K therapy that whenever they talk about Ortho-K you can feel their excitement. It is like seeing them "bouncing off the wall." Parents also proudly share their testimony about how their child's eyesight was getting increasingly worse until they found an Ortho-K solution with us. Whenever we have a nearsighted patient come to our office, we share with them the Ortho-K solution to control the deterioration of their eyes. In some instances, when there is only one parent present, the other parent also needed to be informed. We will invite them to our next upcoming workshop. If they have not been to our office at all and cannot come for the parent-patient conference, we also ask them to attend our educational workshop. We do all the preliminary pre-testing at the workshop. This includes checking their vision through their eyeglasses and getting an estimated current prescription using the automated refractor. This data is sufficient enough for us to discuss the progression of myopia. They will be well informed to make the decision to start the Ortho-K therapy with us. We gain a significant number of new Ortho-K patients at our educational workshops. My presentation is aimed at educating these parents and children on effective use of their eyes and providing them with an effective solution to combat this silent sight-killer disease. It is then followed by questions and answers from the audience. Lunch is provided. Children love these events since they get to be the stars and super heroes of being sight saviors. They get to showcase their Ortho-K insertion and removal skills to other children. We also ordered trampolines and jumpers for them to enjoy. These much-needed public educational workshops are powerful for building a popular Ortho-K practice. Start small; the popularity of your educational workshop will soon spread. At one point, we had as many as 70 attendees. That summer day, as I was delivering the message of "How you can effectively save your child's eyesight for a brighter future," I felt I was truly on cloud nine. The message was delivered. It came across loud and clear. The parents took immediate action and gave their children the greatest gift of all – the Gift of Sight!

Local Newspapers

No one can deny the power of the press. Printed words are immortal. Once a thought, idea, or information is written down and printed, it becomes permanent. The benefit of being an educator is that newspapers are always looking for newsworthy information to publish. You can contact your local newspaper and introduce yourself as a health educator. You have invaluable information on children's eye health that you would like to share in their newspaper. I have experienced that the majority of newspaper welcome this information with open arms. Your information will even give their newspaper the reputation of providing an educational platform on family health. You can even contact the local schools to see if they have a weekly or monthly newsletter that they put out and ask if you could contribute an article regarding the best way to care for youngsters' eyes. I started to write weekly articles for a local magazine in 2005. What started out as a favor to a friend, lasted longer than five years. I must admit; it took quite some time for me to notice results. After a couple of years typing away on the keyboard, people started to mention that they learned about me from this local magazine. Nowadays, there are blogs that many doctors utilize to educate their patients and the public. This is a better and more effective way to go. Anyone can easily search and find your articles online. Once it is uploaded, it will stay for a long time and it will add to your credibility of being the go-to Ortho-K doctor.

Social Media

Of course, you are familiar with the unbelievable influence of social media. The most influential social media are Facebook, YouTube, and Instagram. People absorb everything that is posted on these platforms. They are very effective for delivering a message. It can add toward your reputation when you educate on social media. A lot of successful business companies rely on them. I have not actively sought them out to increase my number of patients. I only use them for about 10 percent of my marketing. You could, however, use it to greater effect if you are more social media savvy than I am.

TV and Radio

In my opinion, radio is the most effective way to get your name out there. People are constantly commuting and you can be right there educating them. I have a weekly radio talk show every Thursday morning. This is the time parents are in the car, on their way to work or taking their children to school. I focus on eye health education. Over the years, my radio host and I have built up a huge fan-base that loyally tunes in every week. These listeners bring their children to Ortho-K therapy with us but still tune in to continue educating themselves on how to improve and maintain the "fit" condition of their children's eyes. You can start your own radio talk shows by calling the local stations and introduce yourself as an eye care specialist who would love to education the public on various topics on eye health. These stations might be appreciating to have health educators on their stations and would love to have you as guest speaker. However, they might ask for some donation to their station. Regardless, the reward of going on live talk shows is enormous!

Occasionally, the local TV station will ask me to co-host a TV talk show with a pediatrician. During Election Day, I was asked to co-host with the mayor of the city to talk about back-to-school eye care in conjunction with the topic of "Changes in Current School System." I feel very blessed to be recognized as a pioneer Ortho-K doctor whose focus is on helping children protect their eyes. This could not happen if I had stopped searching for ways to improve myself and to bring awareness about the danger of the myopic condition when I was already seeing so many patients. I still continue because the message I share still needs to reach more people. It is truly frightening when we look at the alarming statistic of nearly five billion or 50 percent of the world's population that will be inflicted with this thief-of-sight disease by the year 2050. We need more eye care professionals to become Ortho-K experts and to increase the "man-power" in battling this monstrous tornado called myopia! Are you up for it? Let's join forces and change children's lives for better. After all, they are the future of our world.

Chapter 9:

The Implementation of
the Master Plan

"Victory belongs to the most persevering."
– Napoleon Bonaparte

The Introduction to Ortho-K Therapy

U pmost emphasis needs to be placed on providing families with an easy-to-understand education. Above all, you need to provide a service of education without expecting anything in return. Think of it as a way of giving back to society for all the wonderful things that you have been blessed with. I always start my parent-child conference by asking "how I can help," "how can I be of any service to you?" They will tell me that they do not know how their child's eyesight has gone so bad so quickly. I let them explain to me what they mean by "bad"? They will tell me that just 6 months ago she could see 20/20. Now, the nurse sends a note home that she needs glasses. Last week we went to an eye doctor and she said that her nearsighted prescription is -2.00! I was able to see only the big letter size of 20/200. How did it get so bad so quickly?" I then ask them if I could explain to them the causes of myopia. I slowly go through the tips and preventive measures and what they need to do to change their child's current eye use habit. I tell them that these daily changes could help lessen and control the chance of myopia increase. I also add that research has shown that individuals who started to wear nearsighted glasses will have their prescription increase faster from now on. The parents will then ask about Ortho-K. "I don't want my daughter to wear glasses and have the prescription increase every year like her cousin." In a way, they have begged you to start the Ortho-K therapy for their child.

Feel the Pain of Vision Loss

You can understand the phrase, "get a foot in the door." However, have you ever thought how effective it would be if you could get the "message into their mind." But more importantly, let them "felt the pain within their heart." I love to share stories. I like to share my "Why Story."

What was my journey that led to where I now sit in front of you? How did I become the doctor that has helped thousands of children get rid of their eyeglasses and in addition have effectively controlled their nearsighted prescription from increasing? As I look at you, I see my younger self. At the age of 16, I did a horrible thing. I cheated. I cheated on my vision exam at the DMV (Department of Motor Vehicle). I squinted to see the letters during my vision test at the DMV when in reality; I could not see them clearly. Unfortunately for me, I was handed the driver license; the license to possibly get myself killed! That Friday night I invited my friends to the movie. I was driving. I still can see that scene so vividly in my mind's eyes. I was waiting at the intersection on Adam Street, ready to turn left onto Magnolia Street. It was pitched dark. I did not see much or I saw a faint light that I perceived was still very far away. I made the left turn onto Magnolia Street. Suddenly, I felt a loud thunder hitting my tiny Mazda. I opened my eyes a few seconds later. My Mazda was parked on the walkway of Magnolia Street. How did it get here? Slowly, I looked at my car. A big American-made model car hit my car. It was totaled. Kaput! My dad took me to the eye doctor the next day. She said that I have a -3.00 nearsighted prescription and can see clearly only with glasses. That incident not only made me realize how important our eyesight is but how our survival is so dependent on it. At the age of 16, I decided to become an eye doctor to prevent other children from going through what I experienced- a terrifying accident due to poor eyesight.

By sharing my story, the patient and the parents are able to relate to me and they know I can relate to them since I suffer from the same condition. Then, I ask them how I can help. I let them tell me their story of why they need help. What are their goals? What do they want to accomplish with this healthy set of eyes? What do they want to be? Do they want to be a doctor, a lawyer, an engineer? And how committed are they in saving their child's eyesight? Once they hear their own voice stating their goals, their commitment, and their whys, they will acknowledge the need for a drastic change. This works so perfectly well. You do not need to do any convincing. They arrive to the conclusion themselves. Money or cost is no longer an option to consider. We are saving sight; therefore, we are saving lives!

The Mini-Magic Ortho-K Medical Device

Once the agreement is signed and we have completed the Ortho-K examination, I will then proceed to place the order for the custom design lens. The lenses will arrive in about two to three weeks. We make that appointment before the patient leaves the practice. This will prevent the parent from calling the office checking on the status of the arrival of the lenses.

The Insertion/Removal Training

The first day of Insertion and Removal training is very critical. Parents bring their child in with excitement, and sometimes apprehension. They often will not leave their child alone with the trainer. I will have an orientation meeting with the parent. Upmost care has to take place when I deliver this speech. The make and break of a successful Ortho-K therapy starts on this first day. You need to slowly go over with the parents again that their child will have one on one training with an experienced trainer. The parents have to leave the office for one hour or sit aside, not sitting next to the patient. When the patient is left alone with the trainer, he or she can pay full attention to the trainer. This will lead to a speedy and prompt I/R graduation. Parents will not interfere with the training and will not run over holding their child's hand or offer to do it for their child. The child cannot assume that if he or she cannot do it that the parents will do it for them. Parents have nothing to do with this procedure. The patient needs to learn to depend on him or herself. I strongly emphasize that this training is not only training them on the usage of the lenses but training them to be independent in all aspects of Ortho-K care. If mom or dad puts the lenses on for their child then what will happen if mom or dad goes on a business trip for a few days? The patient won't be able to do it themselves and will not use their Ortho-K therapy. Their vision then won't be clear enough for school. Mom and Dad need to let them learn on their own, without giving them any help. The patient's determination to not have to wear glasses is strong. They can and will succeed. We have patients younger than 5 years old who can successfully put on and remove Ortho-K lenses without the help from anyone or without using any removal devices (DMV/ hard contact lens remover/plunger). If, for some reason, the parents sense that this skill is too hard for their child, they may attempt to offer to help. I assure them that their child can do it by themselves; they need to have patience. I also emphasize the importance of bringing them in for I/R training on the scheduled weekly appointment so they can have entire 60 minutes one-on-one with their personal trainer. When patients consistently come on time and are focused, most of them will graduate after two to six trainings. Some patients even graduate after one training!

The Graduation Day

We all make a big deal on graduation day. We take pictures. They get to take the Ortho-K lenses home along with all the supplies of eye drops and One-step hydrogen peroxide solution. They have been trained on all the potential situations that could arise. They learned what to do when the lens moves to one corner of the eye. They learned what to do when eye irritation happens. They learned what not to do when the lenses fall on the floor. Parents get to watch proudly as they get the final instruction before going home and starting Ortho-k therapy that night. The parents' job is to make sure they understand everything so they can supervise the patient at home. The patient is given two tests in our office. The first test is a timed test. They need to put in and remove the Ortho-K lenses within 30 seconds. They need to be confident and proficient with this procedure. If they are unable to do so, they cannot graduate. We do not want them to struggle putting them in and removing them at home before school or before bedtime. The second test is a written test. The patient needs to get 100 percent correct on this test for them to take the Ortho-K lenses home. Simple but important questions are on this test. Sample questions include:

- You need to wash your hands prior to handle the Ortho-K lenses. True or False?
- Why do you need to leave the Ortho-K lenses in the One-step solution for over 6 hours before using it?

Upon passing the test, they are ready to graduate! The patient is then instructed to come back for a follow-up visit the next morning.

The "Wow" Vision

We instruct the patient to keep the Ortho-K lenses in their eyes and come straight to the office the next morning. When the patient comes in, we check to make sure the lenses are in the correct place. We asked the patient to wash his or her hands. Then the lenses are removed from their eyes after the very first night of Ortho-K therapy. Of course, they are curious. They will look up and move their eyes around the room. The first words that come out of their mouths are, "Wow, I can see!" Mom and Dad run over and say, "Really? Read the word on the poster across the room, read the letters on the chart...." The office goes into a "wow vision effect." Everyone is smiling! This is a life changing moment. We get to see it almost every Saturday and Sunday morning. Be honest, do you get that kind of "wow" reaction delivering eyeglasses? Do you feel you have improved lives by doing that? Delivering Ortho-K services will definitely give you that kind of satisfactions.

Chapter 10:

The Fortune Years to Come

"Fortune favors the prepared mind."
– Louis Pasteur

When we are prepared, we reap the reward of not only financial fortune but also the fortune of time and peace of mind. Would it be possible for you to thrive on residual clientele and steady income for years to come? I would answer with a definite, "Yes!" Actually, you have already started building the system that will continue to provide you an additional income from the same patients. Let me explain. In the previous chapters we talked about providing an exceptional, concierge type of service that will have parents and patients rave about you. Not only will they refer you to more of the same kind of new Ortho-K patients, but in doing so they have already decided that their child will stay with you for years to come. They want to come back year after year to take the advantages of the benefits you have been providing to them. They know that their child's eyes were deteriorating prior to seeing you. Since being cared for and coached by you, their child's nearsighted prescription has been stabilized. What would happen if they slack off and stop the Ortho-K program? These children will soon go back to their old unhealthy habits. Their prescription will return back to the way they were before they began therapy. It is like stopping an exercise program once we look slightly thinner. We asked them about their commitment at the first meeting. We tell them that we prefer to work with families who are committed to caring for their eyes long term. This discussion already sets the stage for the years to follow. We also inform them that the yearly maintenance fee is significantly less than the first year. By providing them with this knowledge in advance they are mentally ready to continue their Ortho-K program with us for many years to come. Your fortune will continue for years to come. Instead of spending only the fee of the examination (and walking off with the prescription to be filled online), they will spend on average of \$4,000 -\$9,000 with you to maintain their children's precious potential-million-dollar-earning eyesight.

The Key to a Work-Less-More-Free-Time Schedule

After graduating from professional school, I worked at a Refractive Surgical Center. I felt lucky because I get to work six to seven days a week at the same center. My classmates had to work at two or three practices to make up the 40-hour work week. After working there for a few years, all I knew was work. As a result, my two young children spent more time with their grandmother than with me or their father. Growing up, they did not know who their own mother was. I missed all their important developmental milestones. I was not there when they spoke their first word, nor was I there when they took their very first step in life. It hit me hard one day when my daughter said, "Mom, we never see you anymore!" After hearing those words, I was shocked. I was placing my attention and time on the least valuable things and ignoring those who are the most precious people in my life. I set out to turn my professional and personal life around.

I started to implement the master plan of slowly eliminating insurance companies one by one. I fully focused on delivering the best care for myopic children by offering Ortho-K therapy to all nearsighted patients and young myopic children I came across. I heard people say that all I am about is "Ortho-K therapy, all the time." That is exactly what I wanted to do, to brand myself.

I was asked to go on a live radio talk show to talk about refractive procedures representing the laser surgical that I worked for. It would be an effective way to get my name out there. However, after thinking about it, I refused. If I started out representing a refractive surgical center and then I talked about non-invasive, no surgery, all-natural Ortho-K therapy, and then I would have contradicted myself. To them, I would be known as a hypocrite. My name and true intentions have to stay with what I whole-heartedly believe in – providing the best therapy this world has to offer to our children – Ortho-K therapy.

Within a few short months after enacting the Master Plan and focusing my attention fully on the Ortho-K specialty, my income has increased drastically. I was able to see fewer patients who utilize insurance plans, and I have more free time to devote to perfecting my skills in delivering more Ortho-K care.

I went from working six to seven days per week to about three to four days. Then, for the last six to seven years or more, I worked 3 half-days, which came to about nine to twelve hours per week. By seeing fewer but better-quality patients, my income has increased more than ten-fold. Now, my children get to see their mother all the time. I smiled when my daughter asked me, "Mom, don't you have something else to do; read a book or take a nap?" (What she meant that I hang around her all the time.)

The Flow of a Two-Day Work Week

My practice is open seven days a week. However, I am scheduled to be there only nine to twelve hours per week. Those hours amount to less than two full workdays or 16 hours. I work from 3:30 P.M. to 6:00 P.M. on Fridays. On Saturdays and Sundays, I work from 9:00 A.M. to 12:00 P.M. I work those hours because most of my Ortho-K patients are children. I realized that this schedule works best for them and my practice. As for the rest of the work week, Monday and Tuesday are reserved for my staff to organize the patients' charts that were scheduled that Friday to Sunday. They are instructed to put each and every chart under the "microscope." Inspect it closely to make sure we have answered all their needs and that we have placed the necessary lens orders right away that day. If there is any concern or clarification that needs to be followed up on, my counselor will call parents right away. If they noticed that a patient came with grandma, they will call mom or dad to give the results or give any reminders that was recommended at the Ortho-K examination. Wednesdays are our training days. New Ortho-K patients are scheduled for the I/R (Insertion and Removal) one-on-one training with their coach. Our coaches are highly trained and proficient in I/R trainings. The majority of our new Ortho-K patients graduate the same day, typically with just one training instruction. The first follow up is either Saturday or Sunday morning with me. The eyesight of 20/20 is usually achieved after one night of Ortho-K wear. The next follow up appointment is then made the next weekend (one week follow up); then one month. We see all Ortho-K patients every month or every other month thereafter. We will see them sooner if any complications arise such as dry, red, or irritated eyes. Parents and patients know that they can call us anytime of the day or night in case of an eye emergency. I will see them the same or the very next day. That could be any time or any day of the week. Although, I am scheduled to see patients mostly Friday to Sunday, patients know that I am accessible to them any time of the week if they need me. This gives parents peace of mind that their child is never alone or not cared for if they have eye problems.

The Second Year and Thereafter Consultations

Every Ortho-K practice has different ways of caring for patients. At our office, parents already know that Ortho-K care is a long-term, lifetime therapy. Therefore, our counselor will keep track of when each and every one of our patients' anniversaries come up. Prior to that date, the counselor will inform them of their upcoming renewal due date. They are instructed to come in the office for soft contact lens I/R training if patients don't already know it. After gaining the skill of soft contact lenses I/R, they will wear soft contact lenses for one month or wear their glasses that they have prior to Ortho-K therapy. We will then examine them for the new baseline eye health information. This includes getting their updated glasses prescription, new corneal maps, corneal and retinal eye health (dilation). Thereafter, we will have the one-year parent-patient conference. We discuss all the results. Did the child's prescription increase after one year of Ortho-K therapy? How is the cornea? Do they experience any dryness or redness? What is the health of the retina and IOP (intraocular pressure to screen for glaucoma)? All these data are discussed in detail, followed by a question and answer session. The majority of the time, patients' prescription did not increase but stabilized. In some cases, the prescription has reduced. Parents are often pleasantly surprised to hear that. Mostly, I hear them breathe a sigh of relief when they hear the good news. My counselor will then hand them the agreement to fill out to continue another year of Ortho-K therapy. This system has been put in place many years ago. We keep it because it works beautifully ensuring us the "residual" yearly income that is unheard of with general optometry.

Grow from Patients' Referral Program

Having a large word of mouth referral base is the utopia for any business. We are fortunate to reap the reward of this clientele base. However, don't think that it just comes automatically. Parents and patients for the most part won't mention and refer without having been given the reason to do so. I pride myself in spending a lot of time talking to parents and patients. As you might remember, I love to tell stories. One of the true stories I like to tell is about the power of referrals and it centers on a young man named Tim.

We received a phone call from a mom one day. She asked if she could bring her son in as soon as possible. We arranged an appointment time and we sat down to talk about his eye condition. My first question is always about how I can help improve the child's eyes. She told me that she was at a swimming class. A lady told her to come to see us right away. That lady saw that Tim's glasses were really thick. She wanted to help. Tim's mom was so excited. Why? Because like your parents she was searching for something she did not know existed. She was looking for a solution that could effectively stop or control the ever-increasing prescription of her son. Now, out of the blue, this lady told her about this sight-saving therapy and where to go to get help. She had to start right away. Before she came to us, she remembered Tim's prescription to be about -6.00. After we did the preliminary testing and told her that Tim's prescription has gone to -10.00. She almost had a heart attack! She sat there for a few seconds motionless. I did not know how to handle the situation. But then she burst into tears. It was so heartbreaking to witness this mom's pain!

I told the parent and patient sitting in front of me about the three main reasons why I like to share this true story.

1. It was so unfortunate that the Mom found out about Ortho-K too late; her son's prescription had gone too high. It could have led to serious eye conditions such as glaucoma, retinal detachment, tearing, bleeding. It could have even led to blindness.

2. It was the goodwill of another parent who shared the Ortho-K therapy with another parent. This shows that we care for one another.

3. You are so lucky to have a much lower prescription than Tim. We can surely help you see 20/20 the very next day after using Ortho-K lenses only one night. We have to start the Ortho-K therapy right away. We do not know what will happen in a few months or even a couple of months. Your prescription might go wild on you and just become double!

Tim's story is a sad story. However, an Ortho-K mom referred Tim to us. Therefore, she had saved Tim's eyesight from getting worse. I hope that after we have helped your daughter preserve and stabilize her prescription that you will share this information so someone else's child eyesight will be saved also.

With this story, I have assigned them one of the most important roles of all human kind – the Good Samaritan, Sight Savior, and I've successfully convinced the parent and patient to join our fight against the myopia epidemic.

Chapter 11:

Facing the Obstacles

"The secret to change is to focus all of your energy, not on fighting the old, but on building the new."

— Socrates

Know What the Obstacles Are and How to Overcome Them

When starting an Ortho-K practice, you might wonder about what equipment you would need. If you already have an existing optometric practice you already have the majority of the necessary equipment. A walk through of an Ortho-K patient visit might help you see what equipment is being used.

When conducting an eye examination, you would need an autorefractor to obtain an objective measurement of the patient's prescription. The phoropter is then used to finalize the subjective refractive error and determine the correct prescription. As part of the eye health examination, the slit lamp is used to take a closer look at the different structures of the front and the inside of the eye. An important machine that is necessary to start your Ortho-K practice is the corneal topography. It provides the critical information of the patient's corneal curvature and shape. This data is essential in designing the custom Ortho-K lenses that would mask the precise refractive status of the patient corneal condition. Once all the critical information has been gathered, we can design the custom lenses with the Ortho-K design company. Therefore, the worry of having to buy a lot of equipment was not that important after all.

Where Would the Knowledge of Ortho-K Come From?

I will provide a list of Ortho-K design companies in the directory section. Contact each one of them and they will gladly send you their PowerPoint presentation, user manual, and instructional video on how to use their lenses. Each company will have consultants on site who will guide you on the design of their Ortho-K lenses. Some companies require a certification to use their lens design. It is a very straight-forward and very doable test. Once you read their protocol and user manual, you will be able to pass it with flying colors. Your basic knowledge of Ortho-K can start from here. However, to be proficient in any skill you need to practice, practice, practice, until it become second nature. When I first started fitting Ortho-K lenses, I gave myself a lot of time with each patient; around 15-20 minutes per initial fit. Now it is less than five minutes per patient. This will come with seeing thousands of thousands of Ortho-K lenses on patients' eyes. I believe the most important component for succeeding in your Ortho-K practice is to be your practice's Patient Zero. Then, fit all your staff members, family members, nieces, and nephews. You will know first-hand what potential problems could arise and how to handle them effectively. If you follow the "recipe" outlined in the previous chapters, your first Ortho-K fit should be manageable. As you fit more and more Ortho-K lenses, your confidence will grow.

What are some of the concerns that might come up from family and friends? As you embark on a new journey, you might worry what will your family members, friends, staff members, or your colleagues think about you. In their mind, they might think or questioned why you are "fixing," changing your current mode of general optometry when everything is "fine." Your "Why" will need to be a strong and constant reminder of the reason you needed to change:

- The "Why" is your new path in life to no longer being enslaved by the insurance companies for your living hood.
- The "Why" is the knowledge that could prevent a devastating disease from developing.
- The "Why" is delivering a powerful therapy that could halt or stop the current psychological and physical damage, enabling the healing process for all.
- The "Why" of giving the confidence and improved self-esteem to teenagers when they need it the most
- The "Why" is to see happy faces, sign of relief; and most importantly the appreciative expression in parents' eyes
- The "Why" of us stepping forward to change from ongoing deterioration to providing sight-saving solution

When we focus of all those benefits the doubts, insecurities and the obstacles will disappear in thin air in no time. What is left is the master plan for us to share and care to make a huge difference in lives that we were mean to make.

Chapter 12:

The Conclusion

"We are what we repeatedly do. Excellence then is not an act, but a habit."

– Aristotle

Nowadays, some of the most frequent conversations that we eye doctors discuss among ourselves are about how we work more for less. We feel disillusioned and less fulfilled. We are desperate and frustrated. We have thought about closing the door of our practices and going to work for someone or changing careers completely. I hear it loud and clear!

I was there once. I, too, searched desperately for a solution. I have found an easy step-by-step system that allows me to see fewer patients and still earn significantly more. I wrote this book to share with fellow eye doctors so that they, too, could be confidently able to build a specialty Ortho-K practice that will be profitable and provide more time and freedom for them as well. By building a successful practice that does not solely depend on insurance companies for income you could be able to enjoy your chosen career more. I am confident that I am capable of showing you the way so you can achieve your goals and have all your dreams come true. My dream was to travel the world. Since having an Ortho-K only practice, I was able to travel to Australia, Germany, Canada, Mexico, Japan, and most of the United States. I usually travel one week out of every month of the year!

The easy-step-by-step blueprint can be implemented right away by utilizing all the current resources that you already have. It is best to read instructional manuals from Ortho-K companies, followed by talking to live consultants there to start your first few cases of Ortho-K. Of course, start one case first. Be your own first patient. Increase your knowledge and skills with the people closest to you. Soon, you will be working on your first real patient.

Learn to prepare mentally and physically so that you are 100 percent focused on a successful practice. Acknowledge the power of sharing your message internally within your practice. And you are not alone. When all the members of your Ortho-K team are on the "same boat" with you, you can effortlessly awake the greatness of your efficient high concierge care. Your valuable front line, your staff members are the power house within that can strengthen your message on Ortho-K therapy. This will ensure a constant flow of new Ortho-K patients on a daily, weekly, monthly, and yearly basis. Now, finally, all the vital ingredients are prepared for the Ortho-K blueprint. Use all the available resources to your advantage.

The step-by-step flow of the Master Plan and the implementation of starting Ortho-K therapy for the majority of nearsighted children can be extremely dynamic with the right mindset during the effective parent-patient consultation. Your income will thrive in the years that follow when you implement the process of Ortho-K residual care for all your current Ortho-K patients. It is understandable that all new endeavors will come with possible obstacles and roadblocks. You already have a strong commitment, a rock-solid determination, and the heart of servitude needed to care for all patients.

Therefore, those obstacles and roadblocks are easily being puffed into thin air. Your years of worrying and suffering is about to be over. The making of your specialty Ortho-K practice that will be profitable and provide more time freedom for you is about to become your reality. Now, after reading this book, you can have an accessible career that is totally different, unique, and stress-free from your current situation. My sincere wish for you is to have a prosperous career that you can employ miraculous life-changing care for so many patients to come.

Finally, everything falls into their perfect existence!

Resources to Secure Ortho-K Success

Paragon Vision Science

2120 W Guadalupe Rd Ste. 112, Gilbert, AZ 85233

(800) 528-8279

www.paragonvision.com

AVT (Advanced Vision Technology)

969 S Kipling Pkwy, Lakewood, CO 80226

(303) 384-1111 / 1-888-393-5374

Contex OK Lens

4505 Van Nuys Blvd, Sherman Oaks, CA 91403

(818) 788-5836

oklens.com

GP Specialist; iSee, GOV

15970 Bernardo Center Dr, San Diego, CA 92127

(800) 889-0379

www.gpspecialists.com

Medmont Topography

Unit 5 56 Norcal Road

Nunawading VIC 3131, Australia

+61 3 9259 0800

https://www.medmont.com.au/

Informative Articles

- https://www.questia.com/library/journal/1P3-3949940421/myopia-and-daylight-in-schools-a-neglected-aspect
- https://en.wikipedia.org/wiki/Myopia
- http://www.news-medical.net/health/Myopia-Research.aspx
- https://nei.nih.gov/eyedata/myopia
- https://nei.nih.gov/health/errors/myopia
- http://www.theatlantic.com/health/archive/2016/02/in-2050-half-the-world-will-be-nearsighted/468606
- Why Up to 90% of Asian Schoolchildren Are Nearsighted

- Optom Vis Sci. 2012 Aug; 89(8):1196-202. doi: 10.1097/OPX.0b013e3182640996.
- https://www.ncbi.nlm.nih.gov/pubmed/23380471 Effect of Day Length on Eye Growth, Myopia Progression, and Change of Corneal Power in Myopic Children

Acknowledgements

I would not be where I am today without the constant presence of my supportive mother. I left for optometry school to pursue my dreams when I knew she needed me the most. Because of all the years that she unselfishly took care of our family, I was able to build a successful practice and stable family life. The gratitude and love I have for you, mom, is beyond any words I can describe. This book is first and foremost dedicated to you, mom!

This book would not have been possible without all my wonderful young patients who inspire me to be better each and every day. I have to acknowledge that the greatest gift anyone can receive is the gift of being a parent. As parents, we feel all the pain and joy that our children endure. However, this gift goes a bit further. Being a parent, I am able to feel the sorrow other parents feel when faced with the fear of their children's possible sight loss. It is therefore encouraging me to "reinvent" myself to improve to do the best that I can for all my patients.

The knowledge base of writing a book is there. However, without the constant nagging of my best friend and husband, the words would never be on these pages. I am glad, that even though, I fought it for years, and I have finally settled down and put these ideas to finish this book.

I am grateful for all the three wonderful mentors who took excellent care of me when I was growing up. I treasure all the important life lessons my big brother Vinnie, big sister Wendy, and younger brother Tom have taught me. I am so fortunate to have all of you in my life!

Of course, the greatest present is having you for a daughter, Nikki. Your presence encourages me to the best I can be. Being the youngest in the family you have proven to be the wisest, Dannis. I am proud to call you my advisor! You have made us complete as a family. Of all the education, you both are the two teachers that I have learned the most from. You have positively impacted my life in so many amazing ways! You are the reason I courageously face the world so I can care and protect you each and every day.

The team at The Author Incubator has also asked me to acknowledge the Morgan James Publishing Team: David Hancock, CEO & Founder; my Author Relations Manager, Gayle West; and special thanks to Jim Howard, Bethany Marshall, and Nickcole Watkins.

Thank You

A special thank you from the bottom of my heart!

Thank you for allowing me to share with you my journey to become a profitable and stress-free eye doctor. I truly appreciate the time you spend to read my book. I hope that this book has given you insights into a world that is possible to enjoy a successful and profitable career with an abundant of time freedom. I hope that the tips and strategies can make a huge impact with positive change in your practice. I want you to know that I understand that there was a lot of information in this book and that is why I created my companion program, One-on-One Ortho-K Blue Print Coaching Program. If you would like to work with me and have me help you go through the strategies that I discuss in the book with you and your team, then feel free to reach out and schedule a strategy session with me. You can simply go to Facebook and YouTube and type in "Vuong Optometry" to learn more about us.

You can also contact me at www.drvlc.com or email me at vuongcl@pacificu.edu.

Thanks again! May your future be prosperous and stress-free!
– Dr. Connie Vuong

"Man, often becomes what he believes himself to be. If I keep on saying to myself that I cannot do a certain thing, it is possible that I may end by really becoming incapable of doing it. On the contrary, if I shall have the belief that I can do it, I shall surely acquire the capacity to do it, even if I may not have it at the beginning."
– Mahatma Gandhi

About the Author

D r. Connie Vuong is a licensed eye care physician. She specializes in Ortho-K therapy in Garden Grove, California. At a very young age, she developed an insatiable love for learning by reading relentlessly. The constant reading eventually took its toll. At the age of 16, she experienced a near-death automobile accident that thereafter altered the course of her life. She was diagnosed as having a nearsighted prescription of -3.00 and eyesight of 20/400. It was no wonder that she did not see the oncoming car clearly enough to avoid an accident.

The accident was eye opening for her. It proved that without clear eyesight, our lives can be in great danger.

Now, Dr. Vuong's eye care practice is focused solely on controlling children's nearsighted prescription through Ortho-K therapy. Her patients travel from across the United States, even from as far as Asia, to visit her practice for Ortho-K therapy. An eye care professional for nearly 20 years, she constantly seeks ways to effectively preserve children's eyesight. She realized that the myopia (near-sightedness) is an epidemic that spreads rapidly. As a result, more eye care professionals are needed to combat this sight-threatening disease. Dr. Vuong is committed to increase awareness on Ortho-K therapy to fellow doctors, helping them build specialty Ortho-K practices aimed at preserving children's eyesight for a brighter future!

CPSIA information can be obtained
at www.ICGtesting.com
Printed in the USA
JSHW040545270620
6356JS00001B/22

9 781642 797565